Daisy Days

Daisy Days

Happy Moments
of Seeking and Sharing
By Dean Walley
Illustrated by
Valerie Damon

HALLMARK EDITIONS

Daisy Days

When you wake up

    feeling fresh as a daisy

    and bounce right out of bed

    that means

    you are about to begin...

A Daisy Day!

It really doesn't matter
    if the sky is blue or gray.
The world will seem bright to you...

For it's the sunshine in your heart

that makes a Daisy Day.

Worries scurry away

on a Daisy Day...

And if you laugh
    at little things that go wrong
    that upsy-daisy feeling
    will stay with you all day long.

Some Daisy Days are lazy days

when you have some time

for nappin'...

Or they may be wonderful days

when anything can happen!

Even if the weekend
   is nowhere in sight
   and you have work to do,
   that's all right...

A Daisy Day can make
hard work fun
and earn you praise
for all you have done.

You'll see memories
    blooming everywhere
    and every one will be
    a bright reminder
    of long ago pleasures
    and far away faces.

If there's some secret dream that is

very dear to you...

A Daisy Day

can make it come true!

No matter where you find yourself,

when you stop to look around...

You'll see, to your delight, that
there are Daisy Days to be found.

Daisy Days are full of surprises.
Unexpected "Hellos" can bring a
warm glow...

· Good news in a letter can make you

feel even better!

You may be thinking,

"This day just can't be nicer."

But when you and a friend

share a Daisy Day,

twice as much happiness

comes your way.

It's a wonderful time
   for giving bouquets of love
   to those you think
   the whole world of.

And at sunset,

  when joy is a warm memory
  you can keep forever...

Just remember how easily
a Daisy Day can start — —
you can have one any time at all
if there's sunshine in your heart.